DRAMA LESSONS IN ACTION

a resource book

*****

ANTOINETTE LINE

edited by John Nicholas

twenty five drama lessons

taught through improvisation

DRAMATIC LINES, TWICKENHAM, ENGLAND

Dramatic Lines
PO Box 201
Twickenham
TW2 5RQ
England

A CIP record for this book is available from the British Library

ISBN 0 9522224 2 6

Drama Lessons In Action first published
1997
by
Dramatic Lines Twickenham England

Printed by The Basingstoke Press (75) Ltd
Hampshire England

'I dedicate this book to the children I have shared drama with and the development of their imagination articulated through the spoken word'

Antoinette Line

INTRODUCTION

Drama is great fun and a marvellous tool for learning if used properly and skilfully.

This book has evolved from my long experience of teaching children's drama. Many of the themes are based on feelings as I think feelings are a crucial key to the development of language skills. Drama trains us to understand the needs of others and to develop our imagination and communication skills. In a society where technology increasingly dominates our lives these skills are more important than ever. Yet in today's noise-filled world the spoken word needs to battle to be heard at all.

One of the aims of drama in education is to exercise and develop the imagination and analytical skills. Imagination gives the power to alter and re-create. Mime is of inestimable value in helping to develop natural physical awareness, imagination, clarity of communication, rhythm and awareness of reality. Choral speaking develops voice and breath control by expanding and exploring the group members' expressive voice range and helps to motivate individuals to work as a team and experience a sense of shared responsibility whilst overcoming shyness.

Experiencing and analysing different emotions, learning to communicate more clearly, and interrelating to other people are all aims for a drama lesson. Mime, choral speaking, and characterisation exercises are all structured parts of the lesson leading to improvisation, which can combine all skills in its aim to capture life in its variety of experiences which is expressed through the medium of improvised drama.

Antoinette Line

CONTENTS

SPEECH EXERCISES

These are good for listening and help children to be more articulate.

SPEECH RHYMES

Betty bought a bit of butter
But she found the butter bitter
So she bought a bit of better butter
To make the bitter butter better.

*

Lots of hot coffee in a proper copper coffee pot.

*

Thirty thousand feathers on a thrush's throat.

*

Fingers and thumbs, fingers and thumbs,
Ten fine fellows to help with our sums.
Five on the left and five on the right,
Working together will get the sums right.

*

These are these
And those are those
And these are those
As soon as we change places.

It is a good idea to sit the class at the beginning in a large circle and act in the middle. I use a small bell for order or when I want to give instructions, it saves shouting and children respond to the sound.
I think in an activity like drama children need to know the ground rules.
For example: When you hear the bell please go to your seat to watch the others demonstrate their work.
If you feel children need to quieten down and concentrate begin with these warm up exercises.

WARM UP EXERCISES

1 GRANDPARENT'S FOOTSTEPS One child is the grandparent and stands on his or her own with face to the wall. The remainder of the class stands at the other end of the room and the object of the game is to touch the grandparent without being seen to move. When the grandparent turns around and sees anyone move they go back to the beginning.

2 THE MIRROR Partners face each other and silently copy their partner's movements in turn.

3 TRAFFIC LIGHTS This is a more active game, where each colour represents a movement e.g. black = stand like a scarecrow, green = run, orange = kneel, red = stop, green =go.

4 THE PEN GAME Sit the group in a circle, pass a pencil around imagine that it is something different which has to be guessed. Winner takes a turn.

5 MIME Tossing a coin, bouncing a ball, opening a box etc.,

LESSON 1

THEME SHYNESS

Warm up Mirror in pairs remembering not to touch or talk.
(A) mirrors (B)'s movements, (B) mirror's (A)

Read 'First Day At School'

1 Imagine that you are a shy child in the play ground on the first day at a new school and it's your first play time.

2 In pairs (A) is shy mime playing ball with (B) the outward going partner you had in the mirror scene.
Change roles.

3 In pairs (A) throws the ball and breaks a window in the school.
(B) is a teacher marking books (A) knocks on the classroom door to tell (B) that he/she was responsible.
Change roles.

4 (B) is a shy child arriving to stay with (A) the lively cousin.
(B) knocks on the front door (A) throws open the door.
Change roles.

5 In small groups imagine that you are toys in a toy cupboard.
(a) (A) is a new toy and very shy.
(b) the child/children are asleep in bed and the toys come to life.
Change roles.
Show interesting scenes.

6 In pairs within a large group imagine that you are kitchen utensils, dustpan and brush, knife and fork, salt and pepper pot, washing machine and tumble-dryer etc and one of these items is brand new and feels shy.
The family leaves the house and the kitchen comes to life.
Show selected work and comment.

Reflection Talk about shyness.

FIRST DAY AT SCHOOL

My first day at school today,
Funny sort of day.
Didn't seem to learn much.
Seemed all we did was play.
Then teacher wrote some letters
On a board all painted black,
And then we had a story and .....
I don't think I'll go back.

The Reluctant Pote by Rod Hull

LESSON 2

THEME TIMIDITY

Introduction When we use the word timid we mean quietly frightened.

1 Curl up in a space on the floor. Imagine you are a rabbit that has been locked up in a cage for as long as you can remember. One day the farmer feeds you and forgets to shut the cage. You leave timidly because you have not been out into the world for such a long time.

2 Imagine you are a hedgehog and when you feel timid you curl up in a ball. You are scurrying through the wood when you hear loud animal noises* and react by curling up tightly.
* (selected children make dog, horse, wolf, human sounds)

Read 'The Owl who was Afraid of the Dark'

3 In pairs improvise a scene where the mother bird is teaching a baby bird how to fly.
Change roles.

4 Imagine that you are staying in the country with your aunt. You are in bed and your aunt is asleep. You are hungry and decide to go down to the kitchen for a midnight snack but you feel timid because you are not in your own home.

5 Some people are timid of dogs or cats, others of snakes and lizards, babies, birds or insects. In a space of your own mime in a timid way:
(a) holding a new baby
(b) picking up a huge snake
(c) shooing away a wasp flying around your head

6 In pairs or small groups improvise a scene focusing on being timid:
(a) of an animal or bird
(b) of a reptile or insect
Change roles.
Show selected mimes and scenes and comment.

Reflection Talk about how we can help people who are timid.

THE OWL WHO WAS AFRAID OF THE DARK

Plop climbed out of the nest-hole and wobbled along the branch outside.
He peeped over the edge. The world seemed to be a very long way down.
"I'm not a very good lander", he said, "I might spill myself".
"Your landing will improve with practice", said his mother. "Look! There's a little boy down there on the edge of the wood collecting sticks. Go and talk to him about it".
"Now?" said Plop.
"Now", said his mother.
So Plop shut his eyes, took a deep breath and fell off his branch. His small white wings carried him down but, as he said, he was not a good lander.
He did seven very fast somersaults past the little boy.
"Ooh!", cried the little boy. "A giant Catherine-wheel!"
"Actually", said the Catherine-wheel picking himself up, "I'm a Barn Owl".

LESSON 3

THEME SENSITIVITY

Introduction Some people are sensitive about wearing the colour pink or wearing school shorts and many are sensitive about wearing clothes that are unfashionable.

1 In a space of your own mime being:
(a) an adult who will not wear an article of clothing because it no longer fits
(b) a child who refuses to wear an unfashionable article of clothing
Show scenes and comment.

Read 'The B.F.G.'

2 The B.F.G. is sensitive about his speech, we all feel sensitive about doing things we are not good at. Act out one of the following situations:
playing a piano badly at a concert, falling off a bike or skateboard, failing to hit the tennis ball every time, rollerskating badly, falling over on an ice rink.
Show interesting scenes and comment.

3 Not everyone is sensitive about time keeping, some people worry about arriving late at airports whereas others are often late and even miss aeroplanes. Act a scene in pairs (A) is sensitive about time keeping and (B) is not worried about arriving late:
(a) at the airport
(b) for school
(c) at the theatre
Change roles.

Read 'The People Upstairs'

4 Most people are sensitive to excessive noise. In pairs act out a scene:
(A) has had a party and (B) knocks at the door to complain.
Change roles.

5 In groups of five or more act out a scene where there are noisy people upstairs.
Show interesting scenes.

Reflection Talk about how it feels to be sensitive and what we feel sensitive about.

THE B. F. G.

"Do we really have to eat it?" Sophie said.
"You do unless you is wanting to become so thin
you will be disappearing into a thick ear."
"Into thin air," Sophie said. "A thick ear is something quite different."
Once again that sad winsome look came into the B F Us eyes,
"Words," he said, "is oh such a twitch-tickling problem to me all my life.
So you must simply try to be patient and stop squabbling.
As I am telling you before, I know exactly what words I am wanting to say
but somehow or other they is always getting squiff-squiddled around."
"That happens to everyone," Sophie said.
"Not like it happens to me," the B F G said.
"I is speaking the most terrible wigglish."
"I think you speak beautifully," Sophie said.
"You do?" cried the B F G suddenly brightening. "You really do?"
"Simply beautifully," Sophie repeated.

The B. F. G. by Roald Dahl
Jonathan Cape
reproduced by permission of David Higham Associates

THE PEOPLE UPSTAIRS

The people upstairs all practise ballet
Their living room is a bowling alley
Their bedroom is full of conducted tours
Their radio is louder than yours
They celebrate weekends all the week
When they take a shower, your ceilings leak
They try to get their parties to mix
By supplying their guests with Pogo sticks
And when their orgy at last abates
They go to the bathroom on roller skates
I might love the people upstairs wondrous
If instead of above us, they just lived under us

The People Upstairs by Ogden Nash
first published in Great Britain 1983
under the title 'I Wouldn't Have Missed It'
reproduced by permission of Andre Deutsch Ltd

LESSON 4

THEME LAZINESS

Introduction Some people have a lazy attitude or are lazy about doing some things but not others. A person might be feeling lazy and not want to go for a long walk or dance energetically but might feel like a swim and people sometimes feel tired but that is different.

1 In a space on your own mime in a lazy way:
(a) waking up in the morning, washing, cleaning teeth and dressing
(b) eating breakfast
(c) getting a school bag ready
Show interesting work.

2 In pairs or groups of four improvise a comedy sketch focusing on a lazy family setting off for school or work.
Show funny scenes.

3 In groups of four improvise a scene at school (A) is the teacher and (B) a lazy child. The others are enthusiastic pupils.

4 In groups of four or more improvise a scene at work with a lazy person working behind the counter in a shop, bank or post office. The others are customers in a long queue.
Changc roles.
Show scenes and comment.

5 In pairs or groups of four improvise behaving in a lazy way:
(a) not wanting to get up in the morning
(b) not wanting to go to school
(c) not wanting to join in a game
(d) not wanting to help with the housework or tidying up
(e) not wanting to take the dog for a walk
Show interesting work.

Reflection Ask if the children think that a very lazy person can enjoy life fully.
Follow up reading 'I'm The Big Sleeper' by Michael Rosen
'Time To Get Up' by Robert Louis Stevenson

LESSON 5

THEME DEPENDENCY

Introduction Being dependent on one another is natural but a dependency on the wrong thing can be bad* for example:
smoking, taking drugs, alcohol, slot machines or being over dependent on an influencial friend or group of friends.
* (This could be linked to the School Science/Health Education Policy)

1 In pairs (A) a young child is dependent on older child (B)'s help mime:
(a) (A) finding it difficult to dress in the morning
(b) (A) unable to tie shoelaces
(c) (A) needing to have food cut up small at mealtime
(d) (A) struggling to complete a task.
(e) (A) being too small to reach the top shelf
Change roles.
Show scenes and comment.

2 In pairs imagine that (A) is an old person dependent on younger adult (B)
(a) (A) has the meals on wheels service (B) arrives with the food.
(b) (A) needs to ask (B) to do gardening.
(c) (B) helps to carry shopping for (A).
Change roles.

3 In pairs imagine that (A) is a person dependent on (B)'s help:
(a) (A) is partially sighted (B) is helping (A) to cross a busy road.
(b) (A) is partially sighted (B) is showing (A) around a new flat.
(c) (A) is hard of hearing (B) is relaying a telephone conversation.
Change roles.

4 In pairs or groups of four using examples given in the introduction act out a scene showing that dependency is bad.
Show scenes and comment.

Reflection Ask if the children agree that some disabled people are more independent than many people without disabilities.

LESSON 6

THEME ATTITUDE

Introduction A friendly attitude encourages people to like you and to share with you.

Friendly attitude

1 In pairs mime choosing a present together.

2 In pairs act out a scene shopping for a toy with a friendly attitude (A) is the child and (B) a shop assistant.
Change roles.

3 In pairs mime collecting a toy that was borrowed and has not been returned with a friendly attitude:
(A) knocks at the imaginary door and the neighbour (B) opens the door.
Change roles.

4 In pairs improvise a scene surprising someone special with a birthday party.
Show interesting work and comment.

Change of attitude

5 In pairs repeat 1 and 2 mime choosing a present and act out a scene shopping for a toy but change your attitude. Remember not to fight or use bad language.

6 In pairs (A) in cross mood arrives at a friend's house to return a toy.

7 In groups of four mime having to surprise someone everyone dislikes with an expensive present and very special birthday party.

8 In pairs act out a scene (A) is friendly and (B) is cross.
(a) (A) picks up (B)'s coat by accident (B)'s opening line "That's my coat!"
(b) (A) spills a drink down (B)'s new top.
Change roles.
Show interesting scenes.

Reflection Talk about attitudes and the many ways of looking at the same thing.
Follow up reading 'Maggie and Milly and Molly and May' by E.E. Cummings

LESSON 7

THEME SUSPICION

Warm up Sit and imagine that you are a bomb disposal expert running a stethoscope over an object and then hearing loud ticking sounds.

1 Imagine that you are on a train and you have been called in to investigate a parcel that is thought to be a bomb. This is a dangerous job and you have been chosen for your calmness. Your task is to carefully unwrap and defuse it.

2 In groups of four imagine that you are passengers travelling on a train and one of you suddenly notices an unattended suspicious looking parcel.

3 In pairs mime:
(a) (A) answering the door in a suspicious way to (B) late at night.
(b) (A) is suspicious of (B) a salesman knocking at (A)'s door.

4 In pairs improvise a scene:
(a) (A) the teacher is suspicious that pupil (B) is breaking a school rule.*
(b) (A) is suspicious of the friend (B) over missing money.
* (This could be linked to the School Behaviour Policy)
Change roles.

5 In pairs (A) is a suspicious parent and (B) is a child.
(a) (A) has received a very large telephone bill and suspects that (B) has been phoning friends but perhaps (B)'s brother ran up the bill or the bill might have been incorrect.
(b) (A) asks (B) "Who ate the cake?"
Change roles.

6 In pairs imagine you are staying in the country with your aunt and there is a large cupboard in the house. Sometimes you hear a child's cry coming from inside the cupboard.
(a) (A) and (B) go to the cupboard together and investigate - perhaps it leads to another world?
(b) (A) investigates and (B) is hiding inside the cupboard.
Show interesting scenes.

Reflection Talk about a time when you have been suspicious of someone or something. Were your suspicions justified?

Follow up reading 'Under the Stairs' by Daphne Lister

LESSON 8

THEME HAPPINESS

Warm up Imagine that you are receiving a gift of beautiful flowers or tickets for a sell-out match or concert.

1 Mime happily:
(a) drinking a cold drink on a sweltering hot day
(b) watching a goalkeeper make a brilliant save
(c) eating the most fabulous ice cream desert
(d) skipping through puddles
(e) opening a birthday present
Show interesting work.

Read 'Spring'

2 Mime joyfully:
(a) picking daffodils
(b) watching a newly hatched fluffy chick
(c) smelling pearblossom on a beautiful spring day

3 In groups of four improvise a scene focusing on the joy of the newness of spring and the pleasure of of seeing newborn lambs in the fields, hearing fledglings in a nest and the experience of stroking a lamb, foal, puppy or kitten.
Show suitable scenes.

Read 'How The Cat Became'

4 In groups of four to six (A) is the cat playing the violin and the remainder are bats. Improvise a comedy sketch focusing on the joy and happiness of the cat and the distress of the bats.
Change roles.
Show suitable scenes.

5 In pairs improvise a scene expressing joy and pleasure.

Reflection Ask the children what makes them feel happy.
Follow up reading 'The Grey Horse' by James Reeves
'in Just-spring ...' by E.E. Cummings (selected poems 1923-1958)

SPRING

Nothing is so beautiful as spring -
When weeds, in wheels, shoot long and lovely and lush;
Thrush's eggs look little low heavens, and thrush
Through the echoing timber does so rinse and wring
The ear, it strikes like lightnings to hear him sing;
The glassy peartree leaves and blooms, they brush
The descending blue; that blue is all in a rush
With richness; the racing lambs too have fair their fling.

What is all this juice and all this joy?
A strain of the earth's sweet being in the beginning
In Eden garden. - Have, get, before it cloy,
Before it cloud, Christ, lord, and sour with sinning,
Innocent mind and Mayday in girl and boy,
Most, 0 maid's child, they choice and worthy the winning.

Gerard Manley Hopkins

HOW THE CAT BECAME

Cat was a real oddity. The others didn't know what to make of him at all! He lived in a hollow tree in the wood. Every night, when the rest of the creatures were sound asleep, he retired to the depths of his tree - then such sounds, such screechings, yowlings, wailings! The bats that slept upside-down all day long in the hollows of the tree branches awoke with a start and fled with their wing-tips stuffed into their ears. It seemed to them that Cat was having the worst nightmares ever - ten at a time,
But no. Cat was tuning his violin.
If only you could have seen him! Curled in the warm smooth hollow of his tree, gazing up through the hole at the top of the trunk, smiling at the stars, winking at the moon - his violin tucked under his chin.
Ah, Cat was a happy one.

by Ted Hughes
from How the Whale Became and Other Stories
reproduced by permission of Faber and Faber Ltd

LESSON 9

THEME TASTE

Read 'Hot Food'

1 In groups of four act out the poem.
Show interesting scenes.

2 In groups of four or with a partner mime eating:
(a) an ice cream
(b) a sticky bun
(c) a chewey toffee
(d) hot chips
(e) long spaghetti

3 In groups of four or with a partner mime drinking:
(a) nasty medicine
(b) a drink that is too hot
(c) a drink with a fly in it
(d) a fizzy drink
Show interesting work.

Read 'The Hollywood'

4 In groups of four or more act out the poem.
Show interesting scenes.

Read 'Mrs Utter'

5 In pairs act out the poem (A) is the cat and (B) is Mrs Utter.

6 In small groups mime:
(a) enjoying the taste of a favourite family meal
(b) tasting a lovely dish in an expensive restaurant
(c) eating a school lunch that you detest
(d) tasting something nasty at a dinner party
(e) tasting a bad dish in a restaurant
Show interesting work.

Reflection Talk about favourite and least favourite tastes in food and drink.
Follow up reading 'This Is Just to Say' by William Carlos Williams

HOT FOOD

We sit down to eat
and the potato's a bit hot
so I only put a little bit on my fork
and I blow
whooph whooph
until it's cool
just cool
then into the mouth
nice.
And there's my brother
he's doing the same
whooph whooph
into the mouth
nice.
There's my mum
she's doing the same
whooph whooph
into the mouth
nice.

But my dad.
My dad.
What does he do?
He stuffs a great big chunk of potato
into his mouth
Then
that really does it.
His eyes pop out
he flaps his hands
he blows, he puffs, he yells
he bobs his head up and down
he spits bits of potato
all over his plate
and he turns to us and he says,
"Watch out everybody-
the potato's very hot."

The Hypnotiser by Michael Rosen
reproduced by permission of Scholastic Ltd

THE HOLLYWOOD

We went to this cafe
and I had loads to eat
I had cod and chips.
The cod was huge
and there were hundreds of chips.
Hundreds and hundreds of them.

And I ate the lot.

Then Mum said,
"Anyone want any afters?"
And we looked to see what there was.
There was apple pie.
Don't like that.
There was jam roly poly
Don't like that.
And there was ice cream.
I like that.

There was chocolate, strawberry and vanilla.
I was just about to say,
"I'll have a strawberry ice cream,"
when I saw something else.
It said:
THE HOLLYWOOD

And it was
vanilla ice cream
peaches
cream
chocolate sauce
cherries
trifle
jelly
and
strawberry ice cream.

So I said,
"I'll have a Hollywood."
Dad said,
"He won't eat it.
But Mum said,
"No, no no
if he wants it he can have it."

Dad said
"Waste of money.
He won't eat it.
Mum said,
"A Hollywood, please."
And we waited.

Then suddenly it appeared.
On its own.
Right in the middle of a tray.
With a little paper umbrella stuck in the top.
Everyone in the cafe looked round:
"What's that?"
"That's the Hollywood."
"Oh yes. That's the Hollywood all right."

And the woman put it down.
In front of me.
THE HOLLYWOOD
With the little paper umbrella stuck in the top.

It was huge.
It was taller than me,
And I had this really long spoon
to eat it with,
and now
everyone was looking at me.

I had to reach up
to get to the cherry on the top.
Got it.
In the mouth.
it was lovely.
Then the ice cream
and the chocolate sauce.
Dig in.
That was a bit rich but OK.

Dad loves ice cream and
chocolate sauce
and he's watching me.....
but I don't give him any.
Then there was some jelly stuff
and actually
that wasn't very nice.

Actually -
it was horrible.
Dad said,
"Slowing down, are you?"
Mum said,
"Leave him alone."

Now I was filling my cheeks
so as not to taste it so much.
My hands went hot.
People were looking at me.

Then I got to the trifle.
Soggy cake.
And that was
even more horrible.
I couldn't bear it in my mouth.
I couldn't even put it in my cheeks.
I hunched my shoulders and
I spat some into my hand.
I stopped eating.

Dad said,
"Stopped, have you?"
Mum said,
"Leave him alone."
"I don't like it very much,"
I said.

Dad's hand darted across the table.
"I'll finish it," he said.
You bet he said that.
"I'll finish it," he says.

And Mum turned to me
and said,
"Never mind, dear.
You won't ask for one of those again,
will you?"

I don't suppose I will.

The Hypnotiser by Michael Rosen
reproduced by permission of Scolastic Ltd

MRS UTTER

Poor Mrs Utter
She eats no butter
But gristly meat and horrible pies
With a mug of sour ale
And a loaf that is stale
And a withered brown fish with buttony eyes!

In a black tattered skirt
She kneels in the dirt
And clatters her dustpan and brush on the stairs;
But everything's dusty
And musty and rusty,
For the pump-handle's broken, the broom has no hairs.

The roof-top is leaky,
The window-frames squeaky,
And out of the chimney the fledgelings fly.
Beside the bare grate
Lies old scraggy Kate,
A cat with one ear and one emerald eye.

Poor Mrs Utter
Would mumble and mutter,
"Ah! this is no life for a Princess of Spain.
I once had fine fare
And silk clothes to wear.
Ah me, shall I ever be rich again?"

LESSON 10

THEME TOUCH

Warm up Stand in a circle and imagine that there is an object in the middle. Touch it and respond to its extreme coldness, stickiness, smoothness or heat.

1 Sit in a circle and pass imaginary objects around:

(a) an ice cube
(b) a hot cake
(c) a valuable violin
(d) a feather
(e) a pencil covered in sticky glue
(f) a greasy chip
(g) a heavy box
(h) a cat
(i) a little mouse

2 Stand together in pairs and pass imaginary objects:

(a) a birthday present
(b) a muddy football
(c) a bird with a damaged wing
(d) a heavy box
(e) a favourite cuddly toy

Read 'Touch'

3 Improvise a scene where you are isolating one person.

Read 'The Healing of a Deaf Mute'

4 Improvise a scene where a group of people see a miracle performed by the laying on of hands.
Show interesting scenes and discuss.

Read 'The Feeding of the Five Thousand'

5 In a large group mime the reaction of the huge crowd as Jesus touches the bread and two small fishes and performs the miracle.

Reflection Talk about the effects of isolation on a person and imagine what effect seeing a miracle might have on a group of people.

TOUCH

When I get out
I'm going to ask someone
to touch me
very gently please
and slowly, touch me
I want
to learn again
how life feels.

I've not been touched
for seven years
for seven years
I've been untouched
out of touch
and I've learnt
to know how
the meaning of
untouchable.
Untouched - not quite
I can count the things
that have touched me.

One: fists
At the beginning
fierce mad fists
beating beating
till I remember
screaming
"Don't touch me
please don't touch me."

Two: paws
The first four years of paws
every day patting paws, searching
- arms up, shoes off
legs apart
prodding paws, systematic
heavy, indifferent
probing away

I don't want fists and paws
I want
to be touched
again
and to touch,
I want to feel alive
again
I want to say
when I get out
"Here I am
please touch me."

Touch by Hugh Lewin
from Prison Notes

THE HEALING OF A DEAF MUTE

Then Jesus left the vicinity of Tyre and went through Sidon,
down to the sea of Galilee and into the region of the Decapolis.
There some people brought to him a man who was deaf
and could hardly talk, and they begged him
to place his hands on the man.
After he took him aside, away from the crowd,
Jesus put his fingers on the man's ears.
Then he touched the man's mouth.
He looked up and with a deep sigh said to him,
"Be opened!"
At this, the man's ears were opened, his tongue was loosened
and he began to speak plainly.
Jesus commanded them not to tell anyone.
But the more he did so, the more they kept talking about it.
People were overwhelmed with amazement.

St Mark
Chapter 8 verses 31 - 37
The Bible

THE FEEDING OF THE FIVE THOUSAND

And when the day began to wear away, then came the twelve,
and said unto him,
"Send the multitude away,
that they may go into the towns and country round about,
and lodge and get victuals, for we are here in a desert place."
But he said unto them,
"Give ye them to eat."
And they said,
"We have no money but five loaves and two fishes;
except we should go and buy meat for all this people."
For they were about five thousand men.
And he said to his disciples,
"Make them sit down by fifties in a company."
And they did so, and made them all sit down.
Then he took the five loaves and the two fishes,
and looking up to heaven, he blessed them, and brake,
and gave to the disciples to set before the multitude.
And they did eat, and were all filled:
and there was taken up of fragments that remained to them
twelve baskets.

St Luke
Chapter 9 verses 12 - 17
The Bible

LESSON 11

THEME SMELL

Read 'The Nose'

Warm up Imagine that you are the nose.

1 Mime walking along smelling interesting smells.

2 In pairs develop a dialogue and try to explain how the nose feels.

3 In pairs improvise a comedy sketch focusing on bad smells:
(a) cleaning out a fridge containing an old kipper
(b) visiting a pigsty or stable
(c) trying to locate a bad smell in the house
Change roles
Show funny scenes.

4 In pairs improvise a scene focusing on pleasant smells:
(a) baking cakes for a competition
(b) choosing perfume or aftershave in a department store
(c) arriving at the beach
Show interesting scenes.

5 In groups of three (A) has a heavy cold and has lost all sense of smell mime:
(a) visiting a prize pig in a pigsty
(b) smelling a beautifully perfumed prize rose
(c) tracing a gas leak for (A)
Show interesting work.

6 In groups of four or more improvise a scene titled:
(a) 'I can smell a rat'
(b) 'Do you smell burning?'
Show interesting scenes.

Reflection Talk about favourite smells and find out if everyone likes and dislikes the same smells.

THE NOSE
(after Gogol)

The nose went away by itself
in the early morning
while its owner was asleep.
It walked along the road
sniffing at everything.

It thought "I have a personality of my own.
Why should I be attached to a body?
I haven't been allowed to flower.
So much of me has been wasted."

And it felt wholly free.
It almost began to dance
The world was so full of scents
it had had no time to notice,

when it was attached to a face
weeping, being blown,
catching all sorts of germs
and changing colour.

But now it was quite at ease
bowling merrily along
like a hoop or a wheel,
a factory packed with scent.

And all would have been well
but that, round about evening,
having no eyes for guides,
it staggered into the path of a mouth,
and it was gobbled
rapidly like a sausage
and chewed by great sour teeth -
and that was how it died.

Love Poems and Elegies by Iain Crichton Smith
reproduced by permission of Victor Gollancz Ltd

LESSON 12

THEME SIGHT

Warm up Play blind man's buff standing close together and moving very slowly.

1 Imagine that your torch has gone out deep underground in a cave:
(A) closes eyes (B) moves away and stands still. (A) tries to find (B) without looking.
Change roles.

Read 'On his Blindness'

2 *(a)* In threes: (A) is a blind person shopping in a supermarket and (B) knocks the basket out of (A)'s hand (C) is a bystander.
(b) In pairs: (A) is a blind person shopping at the supermarket (B) is helping.
Change roles.

3 In groups of five improvise a scene (A) is a blind child meeting a group of sighted children in an adventure playground.

4 In a large group improvise a scene at a school for the blind.

Read 'Symphony in Yellow'

5 Sit in a circle, the name of an object is written down and handed to a child.
He/she describes the imaginary object without refering to its colour.
The person who guesses first takes the next turn.
(1) an orange *(2)* scarlet cloth *(3)* a gold ring and silver ring *(4)* a raven

6 In small groups imagine that (A) has lost his/her sight through illness or car accident and has undergone an operation to restore the sight.
Play this scene in two ways, remove the bandages:
(a) (A) recovers his/her sight.
(b) (A) fails to recover his/her sight.
Change roles.
Show interesting scenes.

Reflection Talk about the things that have to be seen to be appreciated.
Follow up reading 'A voyage Round my Father' by John Mortimer
'From Corneal Graft' by Anne Ridler

ON HIS BLINDNESS

When I consider how my light is spent,
Ere half my days, in this dark world and wide,
And that one talent which is death to hide
Lodged with me useless, though my soul more bent
To serve therewith my Maker, and present
My true account, lest he returning chide;
"Doth God exact day-labour, light denied?"
I fondly ask. But Patience, to prevent
That murmur, soon replies, "God doth not need
Either man's work or his own gifts. Who best
Bear his mild yoke, they serve him best, his state
Is kingly: thousands at his bidding speed,
And post o'er land and ocean without rest;
They also serve who only stand and wait."

Milton

SYMPHONY IN YELLOW

An omnibus across the bridge
        Crawls like a yellow butterfly,
        And, here and there, a passer-by
Shows like a little restless midge.

Big barges full of yellow hay
        Are moored against the shadowy wharf,
        And, like a yellow silken scarf,
The thick fog hangs along the quay.

The yellow leaves begin to fade
        And flutter from the Temple elms,
        And at my feet the pale green Thames
Lies like a rod of rippled jade.

Oscar Wilde

LESSON 13

THEME DEAFNESS

Read 'On a Portrait of a Deaf Man'

1 Mime being a deaf person:
(a) walking in the countryside
(b) crossing a busy city road
(c) smelling scented flowers
(d) making a telephone call
(e) eating a meal with family and friends
Show interesting work.

2 In a group of four or six act out a comedy sketch focusing on the problems and frustrations of being deaf.
Show funny scenes.

3 In pairs improvise a scene (A) is profoundly deaf (B) is impatient:
(a) (A) is looking for an item in the supermarket (B) is on the till
(b) (B) a waitress is trying to take (A)'s order in a busy restaurant
(c) (A) is looking around an art exhibition and (B) collides with (A)
(d) (B) is visiting (A) in a school for the deaf
(e) (A) a child is visiting (B) in a mainstream school
Change roles.

4 In pairs (A) mimes an action, cleaning teeth, eating spagetti dressing or undressing, swimming etc and (B) guesses and takes a turn.

5 In groups of three or four act out a family scene.
(a) (A) is jealous of the attention given to the deaf brother/sister.
(b) (A) is deaf and shouts instead of talking without realising and the brother/sister is trying to follow a favourite television programme.
Show suitable scenes.

Reflection Talk about the problems and frustrations of being deaf.
Follow up reading 'Children of a Lesser God' by Mark Medaff
'The Heart is a Lonely Hunter' by C. McCullers

ON A PORTRAIT OF A DEAF MAN

The kind old face, the egg-shaped head,
The tie, discreetly loud,
The loosely fitting shooting clothes,
A closely fitting shroud.

He took me on long silent walks
In country lanes when young,
He knew the name of ev'ry bird
But not the song it sung.

And when he could not hear me speak
He smiled and looked so wise

He liked the rain-washed Cornish air
And smell of ploughed-up soil,
He liked a landscape big and bare
And painted it in oil.

But least of all he liked that place
Which hangs on Highgate Hill
Of soaked Carrara-covered earth
For Londoners to fill.

You, God, who treat him thus and thus,
Say "Save his soul and pray"
You ask me to believe You
and I only see decay.

from Collected Poems by John Betjeman

LESSON 14

THEME LISTENING

Read 'Village Sounds' verse at a time younger children lying on the floor.

1 *verse 1* close your eyes and listen
2 *(a)* squawk, cluck, crow
(b) imagine that you are a duck, goose, hen and cockerel
3 *(a)* bark
(b) imagine that you are a watch dog
4 *(a)* clap out a hammering rhythm chanting din-din
(b) you are the blacksmith hammering horseshoes
5 *(a)* make cycle bell and motorbus noises
(b) you are the postman delivering letters
6 *(a)* grunt
(b) imagine that you are a fat pig
7 *(a)* (A) is the village school teacher and the remainder are school children chanting tables
(b) the bell signals the end of school and everyone runs out
8 you are lying on the village green listening to a favourite tune

Read 'The Deserted House'

2 In pairs or small groups imagine a silent deserted house in the country:
(a) explore silently
(b) hide away and listen out for strangers

3 In fours improvise a scene with a family who never listen to each other. Show interesting scenes and discuss.

Read 'The Listeners'

4 Imagine that you are a traveller knocking on the door of a house and you are visiting people that you haven't seen for a very long time.

5 In pairs or small groups imagine a deserted house where there are magic rooms:
(a) a banquet appears instantly
(b) treasure and gold coins shower down on you from above
Show interesting scenes.

Reflection Talk about the sounds that you might hear in a deserted house if you listen very carefully.

Follow up reading 'Under the Stairs' by Daphne Lister

VILLAGE SOUNDS

Lie on this green and close your eyes -
A busy world you'll hear
Of noises high and low, and loud
And soft, and far and near.

Amidst the squawking geese and ducks,
And hens that cluck and croon.
The rooster on the dung-hill sings
His shrill, triumphant tune,

A watch-dog barks to scare away
Some sudden passer-by;
The dog wakes Mrs Goodman's Jane
And she begins to cry.

And now the crying babe is still,
You hear young blacksmith George
Din-dinning on his anvil bright
Far off in his black forge.

Then on his tinkling cycle comes
The postman with his load,
And motor-buses sound their horns
Upon the London Road.

Sometimes a hay-cart rumbles past,
The old sow grunts and stirs,
And in John Farrow's timber-yard
The engine throbs and whirrs.

Just across there the schoolroom stands,
And from the open door
You hear the sound of 'Billy Boy'
Or else of four times four.

At half-past-three a sudden noise -
The children come from school,
And shouting to the meadow run
To play beside the pool.

And then, when all these sounds are still
In the hot afternoon,
As you lie on the quiet green
You'll hear my favourite tune.

Village Sounds by James Reeves
reproduced by permission of Heinemann

THE DESERTED HOUSE

There's no smoke in the chimney,
And the rain beats on the floor;
There's no glass in the window,
There's no wood in the door;
The heather grows behind the house,
And the sand lies before.

No hand hath trained the ivy.
The walls are grey and bare,
The boats upon the sea sail by,
Nor ever tarry there.
No beast of the field comes nigh,
Nor any bird of the air.

Mary Coleridge

THE LISTENERS

"Is there anybody there?" said the Traveller,
Knocking on the moonlit door;
And his horse in the silence champed the grasses
Of the forest's ferny floor:
And a bird flew up out of the turret,
Above the Traveller's head:
And he smote upon the door again a second time,
"Is there anybody there?" he said.
But no one descended to the Traveller;
No head from the leaf-fringed sill
Leaned over and looked into his grey eyes,
Where he stood perplexed and still,
But only a host of phantom listeners
That dwelt in the lone house then
Stood listening in the quiet of the moonlight
To that voice from the world of men:
Stood thronging the faint moonbeams on the dark stair,
That goes down to the empty hall,
Hearkening in an air stirred and shaken
By the lonely traveller's call.
And he felt in his heart their strangeness,
Their stillness answering his cry,
While his horse moved, cropping the dark turf,
'Neath the starred and leafy sky;
For he suddenly smote on the door, even
Louder, and lifted his head:-
"Tell them I came; and no one answered,
That I kept my word" he said.
Never the least stir made the listeners,
Though every word he spake
Fell echoing through the shadowiness of the still house
From the one man left awake:
Ay, they heard his foot upon the stirrup,
And the sound of iron on stone,
And how the silence surged softly backward,
When the plunging hoofs were gone.

LESSON 15

THEME SECRECY

Warm up Play Keeper of the Keys. Sit in a circle, one blindfolded child in the middle with a bunch of keys in front on the floor. (A) walks around the outside, enters the circle, snatches the keys and tries to leave without making a sound. If successful (A) becomes the new keeper of the keys but if the keeper hears and points accurately the turn ends.

Read 'The Secret Garden'

1 In groups of three improvise:
(a) finding a secret garden
(b) finding a secret room in an old deserted mansion
(c) finding a secret room in your own home
(d) eating a secret midnight feast
(e) spies meeting secretly
(f) a secret society meeting

2 In a large group mime hiding:
(a) (A)'s birthday present from sight by passing it secretly one to another
(b) from the enemy

3 Chinese whispers, pass a long whispered message quickly around the class. 'Tuesday next meet Sam King outside the Theatre Royal at nine fifty three precisely, don't be late and carry a copy of the Financial Times. Sam'll say, "Did you miss the show?" You must reply "Can't stand musicals!"

Read 'Anne Frank Huis'

4 In pairs hold a tense whispered conversation, imagine that you are Anne Frank and Peter and have been in hiding for three years in occupied Holland during the second world war.

5 In a large group improvise a scene focusing on a secret hiding place in wartime.
Show interesting scenes.

Reflection Talk about events and meetings that take place in secret and think why that might be necessary.

THE SECRET GARDEN

Mary's heart began to thump
and her hands to shake a little in her delight and excitement.
The robin kept singing and twittering away
and tilting his head on one side, as if he were as excited as she was.
What was this under her hands which was square and made of iron
and which her fingers found a hole in?

It was the lock of the door which had been closed ten years,
and she put her hands in her pocket,
drew out the key,
and found it fitted the keyhole.
She put the key in and turned it.
It took two hands to do it, but it did turn.

And then she took a long breath and looked behind her
up the long walk to see if anyone was coming.
No one was coming.

Frances Hodgson Barnett

ANNE FRANK HUIS

Even now, after twice her lifetime of grief
and anger in the very place, whoever comes
to climb these narrow stairs, discovers how
the bookcase slides aside, then walks through
shadow into sunlit rooms, can never help

but break her secrecy again. Just listening
is a kind of guilt. The Westerkerk repeats
itself outside, as if all time worked round
towards her fear, and made each stroke die
down on guarded streets. Imagine it -

three years of whispering and loneliness
and plotting, day by day, the Allied line
in Europe with a yellow chalk. What hope
she had for ordinary love and interest
survives her here, displayed above the bed

as pictures of her family; some actors;
fashions chosen by Princess Elizabeth.
And those who stoop to see them find
not only patience missing its reward,
but one enduring wish for chances like

my own: to leave as simply as I do,
and walk where couples drift at ease
up dusty tree-lined avenues, or watch
a silent barge come clear of bridges
settling their reflections in the blue canal.

Andrew Motion

LESSON 16

THEME SCHOOL

Warm up In a space of your own imagine that you overslept and have woken up late, hurridly dress, eat breakfast, clean teeth and leave for school.

1 In groups of three or four improvise a scene arriving at school:
(a) on a beautiful summer's day
(b) on a bitterly cold snowy winter's day
(c) soaked to the skin
(d) (A) has not done any homework and wants to copy again
Show suitable scenes.

2 In large groups of up to ten (A) is the teacher the remainder are pupils arriving late for the lesson and entering the classroom one at a time with an excuse before sitting down and miming until everyone has arrived.
Show interesting work.

Read 'Cider with Rosie'

3 Act out the poem: *(a)* In groups of four at home on the first morning of the new term (A) is the child starting school for the first time today.
(b) In a large group in the playground (A) is the child (B), (C), (D) sisters/brothers and (E) the young teacher.
(c) In groups of four back at home after school (A) is the child (B), (C), (D) sisters/brothers.

4 In pairs improvise:
(a) (A) 'I don't want to go to school ...'
(b) (A) 'I'm not going to school today, no one will ever find out ...'
(c) (A) 'I hate school because ...'
Change roles.
Show interesting work.

5 In pairs or small groups improvise a scene focusing on 'Being Let Down'.
(a) (A) has been let down by a friend who broke an important promise.
(b) Everyone feels badly let down by a popular teacher.
Show suitable scenes.

Reflection Talk about the reasons why a person might not want to go to school.
Follow up reading 'Late for Breakfast' by Mary Dawson

CIDER WITH ROSIE

The morning came, without any warning, when my sisters surrounded me,
wrapped me in scarves, tied up my boot-laces, thrust a cap on my head,
and stuffed a baked potato in my pocket.

"What's this?" I said.
"You're starting school today."
"I ain't. I'm stopping 'ome'."
"Now, come on, Loll. You're a big boy now."
"I ain't."
"You are".
"Boo-hoo."

They picked me up bodily, kicking and bawling,
and carried me up to the road.

"Boys who don't go to school get put into boxes, and turn into rabbits,
and get chopped up Sundays".

I felt this was overdoing it rather, but I said no more after that.
I arrived at the school just three feet tall and fatly wrapped in my scarves.
The playground roared like a rodeo, and the potato burned through my thigh.
Old boots, ragged stockings, torn trousers and skirts,
went skating and skidding around me.
The rabble closed in;
I was encircled; grit flew in my face like shrapnel.
Tall girls with frizzled hair, and huge boys with sharp elbows,
began to prod me with hideous interest.
They plucked at my scarves, spun me round like a top, screwed my nose
and stole my potato.

I was rescued at last by a gracious lady - the sixteen-year-old junior teacher -
who boxed a few ears and dried my face and led me off to The Infants.
I spent the first day picking holes in paper,
then went home in a smouldering temper.

"What's the matter, Loll? Didn't he like it at school then?"
"They never gave me the present!"
"They said they'd give me a present."
"Well, now; I'm sure they didn't."
"They did."
They said: "You're Laurie Lee, ain't you?
Well, just you sit there for the present."
"I sat there all day but I never got it.
I ain't going back there again!"

Cider With Rosie by Laurie Lee

LESSON 17

THEME TRAVEL

Warm up Imagine that you are flying solo in a light aircraft, gently cruising silently through cloud, looking down at the landscape far below.

Read 'The Car Trip'

1 In groups of three act out the poem:
(A) is the mother with two bored children sitting in the back of the car.
Change roles.

2 In groups of four mime travelling:
(a) on a boat at sea in a rough sea
(b) on a coach sightseeing
(c) in a spaceship
(d) on the back of an elephant

3 In a large group mime helping to take part in a search:
(a) for (A), a small child lost on a crowded holiday beach.
(b) (A) is seeking help to look for a little brother/sister lost on the beach.
(c) for (A) lost in a blizzard.
(d) for a child missing on a railway platform.
(e) for an old lady who wandered out of a hospital ward and disappeared.

4 In a large group act out a scene focusing on a search:
(a) (A) is lost in a theme park
(b) (A) is reported missing on a mountain, the weather is deteriorating and the search party must decide to continue or call off the search until the following day.

5 In a large group improvise a comedy sketch (A) is looking for a friend in a large restaurant abroad and cannot make himself/herself understood.

6 In pairs act out a scene focusing on a car breaking down late at night on a stormy night in a lonely place:
(a) (A) is the driver and (B) a frightening stranger
(b) (A) and (B) are travelling together
(c) (A) and (B) discover an abandoned car, the engine is running but there is no sign of a driver or passengers.
Show interesting scenes.

Reflection Ask the children to talk about a never to be forgotten trip.

THE CAR TRIP

Mum says:
"Right, you two,
this is a very long car journey.
I want you two to be good.
I'm driving and I can't drive properly
if you two are going mad in the back.
Do you understand?"

So we say,
"OK, Mum, OK. Don't worry,"
and off we go.

And we start The Moaning:
Can I have a drink?
I want some crisps.
Can I open my window?
He's got my book.
Get off me.
Ow, that's my ear!

And Mum tries to be exciting:
"Look out the window there's a lamp post."

And we go on with The Moaning:
Can I have a sweet?
He's sitting on me.
Are we nearly there?
Don't scratch.
You never tell him off.
Now he's biting his nails.
I want a drink. I want a drink.

And Mum tries to be exciting again:
"Look out the window
There's a tree."

And we go on:
My hands are sticky.
He's playing with the doorhandle now.
I feel sick.
Your nose is all runny.
Don't pull my hair.
He's punching me, Mum,
That's really dangerous, you know.
Mum, he's spitting.

And Mum says:
"Right I'm stopping the car.
I AM STOPPING THE CAR."

She stops the car.

"Now, if you two don't stop it
I'm going to put you out the car
and leave you by the side of the road."

He started it.
I didn't. He started it.

"I don't care who started it
I can't drive properly
if you two go mad in the back.
Do you understand?"

And we say:
OK, Mum, OK, don't worry.

Can I have a drink?

The Hypnotiser by Michael Rosen
reproduced by permission of Scholastic Ltd

LESSON 18

THEME CATS

Read 'The Old Gumbic Cat'

1 In groups of five or six act out verse 2:
(a) (A) is Gumbie Cat sitting still and the mice are scurrying around nearby.
(b) (A) is Gumbie Cat lining up playful squeaky mice.
Change roles.

2 Individually in a space mime being Gumbie Cat:
(a) baking and tossing pancakes for the mice
(b) playing with the curtain cord

3 In a large group imagine that you are playful mice. Hold hands and tiptoe around in a circle (A) Gumbie Cat is hunting and moves about freely. When Gumbie touches a mouse it must move inside the circle immediately and freeze like a statue. Every time a new mouse enters the circle the captive mice adopt a new pose, continue until there is no one left to catch.

Read 'Mrs Reynold's Cat'

4 *(a)* read verse 1 line by line, the children repeating after you.
(b) read verse 2 with selected children taking one line each.

5 You are Mrs Reynold's cat making quiet rasping whistling wheezy sounds.

6 Imagine that you are a cat mime:
(a) cleaning and sitting still as a statue
(b) being a stray stealing scraps from a dustbin
(c) being a pampered pet and stealing tit bits
(d) feeling angry and extending claws
(e) chasing an imaginary mouse playfully in slow motion

7 In groups of four improvise a scene:
(a) the cat has eaten the supper.
(b) the cat is being ticked off for running across the table and knocking over a jug of milk that landed in (A)'s lap.

Reflection Talk about badly behaved cats.
Follow up reading 'The Silent Miaow' by Paul Gallico
'How the Cat Became' by Ted Hughes

THE OLD GUMBIE CAT

I have a Gumbie Cat in mind, her name is Jennyanydots;
Her coat is of the tabby kind, with tiger stripes and leopard spots.
All day she sits upon the stair or on the steps or on the mat:
She sits and sits and sits and sits - and that's what makes a Gumbie Cat!

But when the day's hustle and bustle is done,
Then the Gumbie Cat's work is but hardly begun.
And when all the family's in bed and asleep,
She tucks up her skirts to the basement to creep.
She is deeply concerned with the ways of the mice -
Their behaviour's not good and their manners not nice;
So when she has got them lined up on the matting,
She teaches them music, crocheting and tatting.

I have a Gumbie Cat in mind, her name is Jennanydots;
Her equal would be hard to find, she likes the warm and sunny spots.
All day she sits beside the hearth or in the sun or on my hat:
She sits and sits and sits and sits - and that's what makes a Gumbie Cat!

But when the day's hustle and bustle is done,
Then the Gumbie Cat's work is but hardly begun.
As she finds that the mice will not ever keep quiet,
She is sure it is due to irregular diet,
And believing that nothing is done without trying,
She sets to work with her baking and frying.
She makes them a house-cake of break and dried peas,
And a beautiful fry of lean bacon and cheese.

I have a Gumbie Cat in mind, her name is Jennyanydots;
The curtain-cord she likes to wind, and tie it into sailor-knots.

TO MRS REYNOLD'S CAT

Cat! who hast pass'd thy grand climacteric,
How many mice and rats hast in thy days
Destroy'd? How many tit bits stolen? Gaze
With those bright languid segments green, and prick
Those velvet ears - but pr'ythee do not stick
Thy latent talons in me - and upraise
Thy gentle mew - and tell me all thy frays,
Of fish and mice, and rats and tender chick.

Nay, look not down, nor lick thy dainty wrists -
For all thy wheezy asthma - and for all
Thy tail's tip is nick'd off - and though the fists
Of many a maid have given thee many a maul,
Still is that fur as soft, as when the lists
In youth thou enter'dest on glass bottled wall.

John Keats

LESSON 19

THEME PIRATES AND SAILORS

Pirates

Warm up Imagine that you are pirates on board ship and a fierce storm is brewing.

Read 'One eyed Jack'

1 Imagine that you are a pirate with an eye-patch, wooden leg and a hook for a hand.

2 In groups of four or five imagine that you are pirates on a desert island mime the search for treasure with the aid of a map, compass and telescope.

Read 'Treasure Island'

3 In pairs act out the scene (A) is Long John Silver and (B) a buccaneer who dares to say "I wish I'd stayed in England" to his face.
Show interesting scenes.

4 In small groups act out short scenes you are (A) sailors or (B) pirates:
(a) pirates bind and gag sailors and lock them up in a small cupboard
(b) one sailor wriggles free and unties the other prisoners
(c) the sailors escape to the beach without making a sound
(d) pirates wake to discover that all the prisoners have escaped
(e) pirates search for the prisoners
(f) sailors steal the pirate treasure from a cave
(g) pirates discover that the treasure has been stolen
(h) sailors make an escape in the pirate's galleon
Change roles.

5 In a large group act out the scene you are pirates looking on helplessly as your galleon heads for the open seas and you are all left stranded on the desert island.

6 In a large group form a circle of pirates (A) Long John Silver opens up a treasure chest and each pirate picks up an item in turn and mimes clues. The pirate names the item after five incorrect guesses.

Reflection Imagine what life was really like for pirates and sailors on the high seas.

ONE-EYED JACK

One-eyed Jack, the pirate chief
Was a terrible, fearsome ocean thief
He wore a peg
Upon one leg,
He wore a hook -
And a dirty look
One-eyed Jack, the pirate chief -
A terrible, fearsome ocean thief!

Anon

TREASURE ISLAND

The red glare of the torch, lighting up the interior of the blockhouse, showed me the worst of my apprehensions realized.
The pirates were in possession of the house and stores;
there was the cask of cognac, there were the pork and bread, as before;
and, what tenfold increased my horror, not a sign of any prisoner.
I could only judge that all had perished, and my heart smote me sorely that I had not been there to perish with them.

There were six of the buccaneers, all told; not another man was left alive. Five of them were on their feet, flushed and swollen, suddenly called out of the first sleep of drunkenness. The sixth had only risen upon his elbow: he was deadly pale, and the blood-stained bandage round his head told that he had recently been wounded, and still more recently dressed.
I remembered the man who had been shot and had run back among the woods in the great attack, and doubted not that this was he.

The parrot sat, preening her plumage, on Long John's shoulder.
He himself, I thought, looked somewhat paler and more stern than I was used to. He still wore the fine broadcloth suit in which he had fulfilled his mission, but it was bitterly the worse for wear, daubed with clay and torn with the sharp briers of the wood.

Robert Louis Stevenson

Sailors

Warm up Imagine that you are sailors on board ship and you see a pirate ship appear on the horizon and realise that it is heading towards you.

Read 'The Tempest'

1 In groups of five imagine that you are sailors aboard a galleon caught in a terrible storm, the ship is wrecked and you are swept ashore.

2 In groups of three improvise a scene focusing on a magic island and Prospero, a magician and his daughter/son who live there cut off from the world. The child stumbles across a shipwrecked sailor and takes him to the father who gives the sailor a magic potion.
Show interesting scenes.

3 In pairs mime: *(a)* (A) is Prospero and (B) Ariel, a spirit making magic.
(b) Prospero has warned (A) the sailor never to enter the huge cave on the shore but the sailor finds himself drawn there and enters it with (B) a friend.
Change parts.

4 In a large group mime: (A) and (B) are terrified sailors inside the cave.
(a) (A) and (B) walk down a long winding tunnel with walls that move.
(b) (A) and (B) face writhing snakes in a snake pit.
(c) (A) and (B) escape from the snake pit and continue down the tunnel to a place where slow moving monsters attempt to block their path.
(d) (A) and (B) see huge spiders and discover a crumbling staircase that leads upwards out of the cave into daylight where seagulls circle overhead.

5 In a large group (A) is a shipwrecked sailor exploring a magic island mime:
(a) (A) stumbles across fearsome dragons, poisonous snakes and huge birds that swoop down threateningly.
(b) (A) comes across groups of shy dragons, harmless snakes and doves.
Show interesting work.

Reflection Ask how living in total isolation might change a person.
Follow up reading 'The Witches Ride' by Karla Kuskin
'Sorcerer' by Clive Sansom

THE TEMPEST

If by your art, my dearest father, you have
Put the wild waters in this roar, allay them:
The sky, it seems, would pour down stinking pitch,
But that the sea, mounting to the welkin's cheek,
Dashes the fire out. 0, I have suffer'd
With those that I saw suffer! a brave vessel,
Who had, no doubt, some noble creature in her,
Dash'd all to pieces. 0, the cry did knock
Against my very heart! poor souls! they perish'd.
Had I been any god of power, I would
Have sunk the sea within the earth, or e'er
It should the good ship so have swallow'd, and
The fraughting souls within her.

The Tempest act I scene I
William Shakespeare

LESSON 20

THEME FIFTH OF NOVEMBER AND HALLOWEEN

Fifth of November

Read 'The Remarkable Rocket'

1 In pairs develop a dialogue and try to explain how the rocket feels.

2 On your own in a space imagine that you are a firework.

3 In groups of four imagine that you are a firework with a big personality
(A) the Roman candle is happy (B) the Rocket is cross
(C) the Sparkler is excitable (D) the Volcano is proud and dignified
(a) You are standing tall and straight in line and each is lit in turn.
(b) You are all lit at the same time.
(c) (B) is damp and will not light.
Show interesting work.

4 In a large group act out a scene focusing on a damp rocket at the firework display.

5 In groups of five or six curl up on the floor in a circle and imagine that you are a fire. Begin by repeating 'crack-spark' grow tall and stretch high repeat 'flame-fire' and repeat 'ashes' as you die down and silently burn out.

6 Curl up in a space on the floor and imagine that you are a squirrel in the woods woken from sleep on firework night.
(bang a drum to make firework noises and flick light switches on and off)

7 Imagine that you are alone in the woods on firework night mime being:
(a) an alert owl perched high in a tree
(b) a hungry fox
(c) a lost cat/dog
(d) a frightened rabbit
(e) a lost child
In pairs talk about how you felt and how you reacted to the fireworks.

Reflection Ask the children what they think about fireworks.

THE REMARKABLE ROCKET

The Rocket was very damp, so he took a long time to burn.
At last, however, the fire caught him.
"Now I am going off!" he cried, and he made himself very stiff and straight.
"I know I shall go much higher than the stars, much higher than the moon,
much higher than the sun. In fact, I shall go so high that ..... "
Fizz ! Fizz ! Fizz ! and he went straight up into the air.
"Delightful!" he cried, 'I shall go on like this for ever. What a success I am!"
But nobody saw him.
Then he began to feel a curious tingling sensation all over him.
"Now I am going to explode," he cried.
"I shall set the whole world on fire, and make such a noise that nobody
will talk about anything else for a whole year."
And he certainly did explode.
Bang ! Bang ! Bang ! went his gunpowder. There was no doubt about it.
But nobody heard him, not even the two little boys, for they were fast asleep.
Then all that was left of him was the stick,
and this fell down on the back of a Goose who was taking a walk by the
side of the ditch.
"Good heavens!" cried the Goose. "It is going to rain sticks," and she rushed
into the water.
"I knew I should create a great sensation," gasped the Rocket,
and he went out.

Oscar Wilde

LESSON 20

Halloween

Warm up Form a circle and imagine that you are witches/wizards with a foul smelling bubbling cauldron hanging over a fire in the middle.

Read 'Macbeth'

1 Circle around the cauldron chanting quietly 'Double, double, toil and trouble; fire burn, and cauldron bubble'

2 In a large group form a circle (A) the witch/wizard chooses an apprentice to fetch an ingredient for the spell:
(a) 'Find me a toad' (B) finds a toad and places it in the cauldron and the apprentices circle making the magic 'oo' sound
(b) 'Find me a spider' (C) finds a spider and places it in the cauldron and the apprentices circle making the magic 'oh' sound
(c) 'Find me a snake' (D) finds a snake and places it in the cauldron and the apprentices circle making a magic 'aw' sound
(d) 'Find me a bat' (E) finds a bat and places it in the cauldron and the apprentices circle making a magic 'ah' sound
(e) 'Find me a fly' (F) finds a fly and places it in the cauldron and the apprentices circle making a magic 'ay' sound
(f) 'Find me a beetle' (G) finds a beetle and places it in the cauldron and the apprentices circle making a magic 'ee' sound

3 In a large circle creeping around the cauldron mime:
(a) tasting the magic potion which then slows down your movements
(b) drinking a little of the magic potion which speeds up your movements
(c) drinking more of the magic potion and falling asleep on your feet

4 In small groups imagine that you are witches/wizards improvise a scene:
(a) in a witches/wizard's repair shop.
(b) in a witch's/wizard's restaurant.

Read 'Chip the Glasses and Crack the Plates'

5 In groups of four act out the poem.

Reflection Talk about the poem.

MACBETH

Round about the cauldron go;
In the poison'd entrails throw.
Toad, that under cold stone,
Days and nights hast thirty-one
Swelter'd venom sleeping got,
Boil thou first i' the charmed pot!
Double, double, toil and trouble;
Fire burn, and cauldron bubble.

Macbeth act IV scene I
William Shakespeare

CHIP THE GLASSES AND CRACK THE PLATES

Chip the glasses and crack the plates!
Blunt the knives and bend the forks!
That's what Bilbo Baggins hates -
Smash the bottles and burn the corks.

Cut the cloth and tread on the fat!
Pour the milk on the pantry floor!
Leave the bones on the bedroom mat!
Splash the wine on every door!

Dump the crocks in a boiling bowl
Pound them with a thumping pole
And when you've finished, if any are whole,
Send them down the hall to roll.

That's what Bilbo Baggins hates!
So carefully! carefully with the plates

LESSON 21

THEME AUTUMN

Read 'Autumn'

1 In groups of four act out the frustration of not going out to play because the weather is wet and windy.
Show interesting scenes.

2 In groups of four imagine you are out on a blustery day mime:
(a) being blown along by strong gusts of wind
(b) (A)'s hat is blowing away in the wind and everyone chases after it
(c) trying to stop the umbrella turning inside out
Show interesting work.

3 Imagine that you are a tree in a forest with branches shaking in the wind.

4 Imagine that you are a leaf falling from a tree and repeat the word:
(a) 'down' as you flutter slowly to the ground
(b) *(1)* 'tumble' *(2)* ' bumble' or *(3)* 'crumble' and spiral slowly
(c) *(1)* 'red' *(2)* 'yellow' or *(3)* 'brown' and spiral very slowly
(d) 'flitter-skitter' and spiral very slowly at first growing faster and faster

5 In groups of five or six repeat 4*(a)* - *(d)* spiralling close together.

6 Individually in a space imagine that you are the wind.
Blow gently and grow fierce before finally dying away completely.

7 One at a time sitting in a circle:
(a) use a word to describe something about Autumn that you really like.
(b) use a word to describe something about Autumn that you dislike.

8 Individually mime walking through the woods:
(a) catching falling leaves
(b) kicking up fallen leaves

Reflection Talk about the seasons and how weather affects mood.
Follow up reading 'October' by Rose Fyleman
'Autumn Leaves' by Eve Merriam
'Bonfire' by Jean Kenwood

AUTUMN

I love the fitful gust that shakes
The casement all the day,
And from the glossy elm-tree takes
The faded leaves away,
Twirling them by the window pane
With thousand others down the lane.

I love to see the shaking twig
Dance till the shut of eve,
The sparrow on the cottage rig,
Whose chirp would make believe
That Spring was just now flirting by
In Summer's lap with flowers to lie.

I love to see the cottage smoke
Curl upwards through the trees,
The pigeons nestled round the cote
On November days like these;
The cock upon the dunghill crowing,
The mill-sails on the heath a-going.

The feather from the raven's breast
Falls on the stubble lea,
The acorns near the old crow's nest
Drop pattering down the tree;
The grunting pigs, that wait for all,
Scramble and hurry where they fall.

John Clare from A Book of a Thousand Poems

LESSON 22

THEME CHRISTMAS

Warm up Imagine that you are a tree with boughs heavily laden with snow standing in a dark silent forest.

Read 'The Spider's Christmas'

1 On your own in a space imagine that you are the kindly old widow:
(a) cleaning and sweeping away cobwebs and shooing spiders from the corners of the cottage
(b) choosing a Christmas tree deep in the forest and digging it up
(c) carrying the tree back home
(d) making a special present for a friend or pet
(e) wrapping up presents
(f) baking lots of shortbread biscuits to hang on the tree
(g) carefully decorating the Christmas tree
Show interesting work.

2 In a large group imagine that you are excited village children act out a scene:
(a) hurrying through the forest to the widow's cottage on Christmas Eve.
(b) (A) is the kindly old widow welcoming you to her little cottage.

3 In a large group mime:
(a) (A) is Christkindel opening the cottage door to spiders of every size and type who scurry across the floor and up into the branches of the tree.
(b) (A) is Christkindel transforming spiders web, hold hands and form lines of silver and gold thread that stretch out and wrap around the tree.

4 Mime on your own in a space imagine that you are the kindly old widow waking up to see the tree covered in silver and gold threads.

5 In a large circle imagine that you are village children sitting around the beautiful Christmas tree in the kindly old widow's little cottage.
Make a Christmas wish out loud in turn.

Reflection Talk about Christmas wishes and the magic of Christmas.
Follow up reading 'Little tree' by E.E. Cummings

THE SPIDER'S CHRISTMAS

It was Christmas Eve morning, and the old cockerel crowed lustily
at first light. The kindly old widow who lived on the far side of the forest
woke with a start; there was so much to be done and so little time
in which to do it.
First she cleaned every room in her cottage thoroughly, taking great care
to sweep away the cobwebs from the narrowest of narrow cracks in the
walls and the darkest of dark corners. Eventually, she felt satisfied
that all the spiders had been swept away and that there wasn't
a single spider or cobweb to be found anywhere in her home.
Then she wrapped up against the bitter cold and trudged through deep snow
into the heart of the forest in search of a Christmas tree. She chose carefully
and carried the tall straight pine tree back home to decorate.
The kindly widow baked shortbread stars and hung them with scarlet
ribbons from the branches of the tree and laid presents that she had made
herself beneath the tree on the polished wooden floor. There was a gift
for every child in the village, and something special for her cat,
the old cockerel and all the hens. She'd remembered everyone,
no one had been forgotten.....
except for the spiders, because they had been swept away.
The village children arrived at the cottage after dark. They sang carols
and the widow invited them in and gave each excited child a shortbread
star and a carefully wrapped present. The children laughed and chattered,
admired the beautiful Christmas tree and wondered what presents
Christkindel would bring next morning.
The kindly widow found herself caught up in the excitement and she
made a Christmas wish. She closed her eyes and very quietly repeated the
wish that something magical might happen that same night three times over.
Then she thought nothing more of it and the village children went home.
After the widow had fallen asleep spiders began to gather outside the
front door of the cottage. They were longing to catch a glimpse of the
beautiful Christmas tree but had been shut outside in the bitter cold
and needed help if they were to get back inside the cottage.

The spiders waited patiently. At last Christkindel passed by on his way
to take presents to the village children. He took pity on the spiders
and opened the cottage door a crack ...... and let them all in.
Tiny spiders, huge spiders, smooth spiders, hairy and spotted spiders,
brown, black, red and yellow spiders and the palest of pale
see-through spiders came creeping, crawling, sneaking softly, scurrying
and hurrying, zigging-zagging, weaving, wobbling, silently
over the doorstep into the old widow's spick and span cottage.
The curious spiders crept and crawled closer and closer
and closer to the Christmas tree and before Christkindel had time
to stop them they had all disappeared upwards and scurried and hurried
running helter skelter to and fro swinging and dangling
from branch to branch by their silk threads leaving a tangled trail of cobwebs.
Christkindel knew that the kindly old widow would be upset to see the tree
smothered in cobwebs because she had worked hard to clean her cottage
and sweep away the spiders and cobwebs so he touched the silk thread
and the cobwebs were changed to gold and silver.
The widow was spellbound when she saw the glittering tree on Christmas
morning.
And from that day on she left cobwebs in all the corners of the little cottage
to allow the spiders to share her celebrations; and she hung gold and silver
tinsel on the tree every year as a reminder of that magical Christmas Eve
when her own Christmas wish had been granted.

The Spider's Christmas
retold by Heather Stephens

LESSON 23

THEME CHANGE

Read 'The Cloud Mobile'

1 Re-read line by line and in groups of three to six mime being:
verse 1 continents, countries or seas forming, shrinking and fading away
2 small islands changing shape quickly or slowly
3 seas flooding across land, hills emerging from a flood
4 hard angular shapes and soft shapes moving quickly or slowly
(Clap hands to freeze and unfreeze movement throughout the poem)
Show imaginative work.

Read 'The Frog and the Golden Ball'

2 Act out the poem.
(a) In pairs (A) is the Prince (B) the Princess
(b) In fours with (A) the Prince (B) the Princess, King and Queen

Read 'The Christmas Carol'

3 In pairs improvise a scene titled 'Scrooge has a change of heart'.

4 In a large group form a circle with Scrooge sitting on a chair in the middle. People from his past and present walk around slowly and step forward one at a time to shame Scrooge by reminding him of his meanness.

5 In pairs act out a scene at the cinema (B) is a young child sitting on a seat (A) asks (B) to change places and (B) refuses.
(1) the situation is resolved amicably.
(2) the situation cannot be resolved.

6 In fours act out a scene in a residential home for the elderly (A) asks (B) to pass a newspaper and (B) refuses.
(1) everyone becomes involved and the situation is resolved.
(2) the situation cannot be resolved.
Change roles.

7 In a large group improvise a picnic scene focusing on a change in weather. Show interesting scenes.

Reflection Talk about the many ways in which different things change.

THE CLOUD MOBILE

Above my face is a map.
Continents form and fade.
Blue countries, made
on a white sea, are erased,
and white countries traced
on a blue sea.

It is a map that moves,
faster than real, but so slow.
Only my watching proves
that island has being,
or that bay.

Coasts cracking,
the ocean spills over,
then new hills
heap into view
with river-cuts of blue
between them.

It is a map of change.
This is the way things are
with a stone or a star.
This is the way things go,
hard or soft,
swift or slow.

May Swenson

THE FROG AND THE GOLDEN BALL

She let her golden ball fall down the well
And begged a cold frog to retrieve it
For which she kissed his ugly, gaping mouth -
Indeed, he could scarce believe it.

And seeing him transformed to his princely shape,
Who had been by hags enchanted,
She knew she could never love another man
Nor by any fate be daunted.

But what would her royal father and mother say?
They had promised her in marriage
To a cousin whose wide kingdom marched with theirs,
Who rode in a jewelled carriage.

"Our plight, dear heart, would appear past human hope
To all except you and me: to all
Who have never swum as a frog in a dark well
Or have lost a golden ball."

"What then shall we do now?" she asked her lover.
He kissed her again, and said
"Is magic of love less powerful at your Court
Than at this green well-head?"

THE CHRISTMAS CAROL 1

At length the hour of shutting up the counting-house arrived.
With an ill will Scrooge dismounted from his stool
and tacitly admitted the fact to the expectant clerk in the Tank,
who instantly snuffed his candle out and put on his hat.
"You'll want all day tomorrow, I suppose?" said Scrooge.
"If quite convenient, sir."
"It's not convenient," said Scrooge, "and it's not fair.
If I was to stop half a crown for it, you'd think yourself ill used, I'll be bound?"
The clerk smiled faintly.
"And yet," said Scrooge, "you don't think me ill used,
when I pay a day's wages for no work."
The clerk observed that it was only once a year.
"A poor excuse for picking a man's pocket every twenty-fifth of December!"
said Scrooge, buttoning his greatcoat to the chin.
"But I suppose you must have the whole day.
Be here all the earlier next morning!"
The clerk promised that he would; and Scrooge walked out with a growl.
The office was closed in a twinkling, and the clerk,
with the long ends of his white comforter dangling below his waist
(for he boasted no greatcoat), went down a slide on Cornhill,
at the end of a line of boys, twenty times,
in honour of it's being Christmas Eve, and then ran home to Camden Town
as hard as he could pelt, to play at blind man's buff.

THE CHRISTMAS CAROL 11

Scrooge was better than his word. He did it all, and infinitely more;
and to Tiny Tim, who did not die, he was a second father. He became
as good a friend, as good a master, and as good a man, as the good old City
knew, or any other good old city, town , or borough, in the good old world.
Some people laughed to see the alteration in him, but he let them laugh
and little heeded them; for he was wise enough to know that nothing
ever happened on this globe for good, at which some people did not have
their fill of laughter in the outset; and knowing that such as these
would be blind anyway, he thought it quite as well that they should
wrinkle up their eyes in grins, as have the malady in less attractive forms.
His own heart laughed: and that was quite enough for him.

Charles Dickens

LESSON 24

THEME THE SEA

Warm up Individually find a space and move like the sea.

1 Mime, in a large group standing in line:
(a) become rolling waves by holding hands and moving arms gently.
(b) hold an imaginary shell up to the ear and listen to
the sound of the sea before making the sound and passing on the shell.

2 In groups of four improvise a scene:
(a) 'Ghosts from a sea wreck'.
(b) 'Opening a treasure chest found in an old wreck'.
(c) 'Unleashing the genie from a bottle washed up on the beach'.

Read 'The Fisherman and his Soul'

3 Lie on the floor with closed eyes and imagine that you have fallen asleep and find yourself changing into a huge sea creature, you are now breathing through gills, your green-blue skin is cold and wet to the touch:
(a) wake slowly and move around your underground cavern.
(b) make your way upwards until you reach the surface of the sea.
(c) sink back down to the seabed repeating the sound 'Shhh' and sleep.
Show interesting work.

4 In pairs improvise a scene (A) is a fisherman (B) a mermaid/sea creature.

Read 'The Lobster Quadrille'

5 Choose individuals to read 1 line each, the group recites the choruses:
Verse 1 'Will you, won't you, ... will you join the dance? ....
2 'Would not, could not, ... would not join the dance....
3 'Will you, won't you, ... will you join the dance?.........

6 In groups of five or more improvise a comedy sketch centering around the story of the porpoise following the whiting who is trying to persuade a snail to join lobsters and turtles dancing on the beach (A) whiting (B) snail (C) porpoise (D) lobster/lobsters (E) turtle/turtles.
Show funny scenes.

Reflection Talk about the moods of the sea.
Follow up reading 'The Sea' by James Reeves
'Old Man Ocean' by Russell Hoban

THE FISHERMAN AND HIS SOUL

Every evening the young Fisherman went out upon the sea,
and threw his nets into the water.

When the wind blew from the land he caught nothing, or but little at best,
for it was a bitter and black-winged wind, and rough waves rose up to meet it.
But when the wind blew to the shore, the fish came in from the deep,
and swam into the meshes of his nets, and he took them to the market-place
and sold them.

Every evening he went out upon the sea, and one evening the net was so heavy
that hardly could he draw it into the boat.
And he laughed, and said to himself,
"Surely I have caught all the fish that swim, or snared some dull monster
that will be a marvel to men, or something of horror that the great Queen
will desire",
and putting forth all his strength, he tugged at the coarse ropes till,
like lines of blue enamel round a vase of bronze, the long veins rose up
on his arms.
He tugged at the thin ropes, and nearer and nearer came the circle of flat corks,
and the net rose at last to the top of the water.

But no fish sat in it, nor any monster or thing of horror,
but only a little Mermaid lying fast asleep.

Oscar Wilde

THE LOBSTER QUADRILLE

"Will you walk a little faster?" said a whiting to a snail,
"There's a porpoise close behind us, and he's treading on my tail.
See how eagerly the lobsters and the turtles all advance!
They are waiting on the shingle - will you come and join the dance?
Will you, won't you, will you, won't you, will you join the dance?
Will you, won't you, will you, won't you, won't you join the dance?"

"You can really have no notion how delightful it will be
When they take us and throw us, with the lobsters, out to sea!"
But the snail replied "Too far, too far!" and gave a look of askance -
Said he thanked the whiting kindly, but he would not join the dance.
Would not, could not, would not, could not, would not join the dance.
Would not, could not, would not, could not, could not join the dance.

"What matters it how far we go?" his scaly friend replied.
"There is another shore, you know, upon the other side.
The further off from England the nearer is to France -
Then turn not pale, beloved snail, but come and join the dance.
Will you, won't you, will you, won't you, will you join the dance?
Will you, won't you, will you, won't you, won't you join the dance?"

Lewis Carroll

LESSON 25

THEME MAGIC

Warm up Imagine that you are a person with special powers, conjure up a magic castle in the air with spiralling staircases and fantastic turrets. Explore the castle, dismantle it or click your fingers to make it vanish at dusk.

Read 'A Wizard of Earthsea'

1 Imagine the desolate scene and mime in pairs:
(a) (A) is the wizard/witch loosing the power of magic and (B) the ghost absorbing power and growing stronger.
(b) the boat capsizes (A) is thrown into the icy water (B) hovers closeby.
(c) (A) is washed ashore on a strange desolate island and (B) shadows the wizard/witch's movements.
Change roles.

2 In a large group imagine that you are beady eyed witches/wizards act out:
(a) flying on broomsticks sweeping through the night quietly humming shrill discordant notes.
(b) circling around a cauldron *(1)* silently *(2)* humming a single note *(3)* making the magic 'aaahhh' sound.

3 Imagine that you are a witch/wizard alone on the night of a full moon:
(a) fly to the moon and bring back unique items of value *(1)* moon dust *(2)* a moonbeam *(3)* a moon crystal *(4)* moon dew.
(b) destroy a gloomy forest and conjure up an ice palace, light candles inside and marvel at the magical light reflected in thousands of mirrors
Show interesting work.

4 Imagine an overgrown deserted palace, in a large group act out the scene:
(A) the witch/wizard discovers people who have been sleeping for a hundred years and wakes them.

5 In pairs imagine that you are a sorcerer and sorcerer's apprentice mime conjuring up magic birds in a curious and amusing way.
Change roles.

Reflection Talk about the spells that you would like to cast and say why.

Follow up reading 'The Witches Ride' by Karla Kuskin
'Sorcerer' by Clive Sansom

A WIZARD OF EARTHSEA

He turned the boat around, working her carefully round with spell
and with makeshift oar lest she knock up against the underwater rocks
or be entangled in the outreaching roots and branches,
till she faced outward again; and he was about to raise up a wind
to take him back as he had come, when suddenly the words of the spell
froze on his lips, and his heart went cold within him.
He looked back over his shoulder.
The shadow stood behind him in the boat.

Had he lost one instant, he had been lost; but he was ready,
and lunged to seize and hold the thing which wavered and trembled there
within arm's reach. No wizardry would serve him now,
but only his own flesh, his life itself, against the unliving.
He spoke no word, but attacked, and the boat plunged
and pitched from his sudden turn and lunge.
And a pain ran up his arms into his breast, taking away his breath,
and an icy cold filled him, and he was blinded; yet in his hands
that seized the shadow there was nothing - darkness, air.

Excerpt from A Wizard of Earthsea
by Ursula K. LeGuin

ADDITIONAL TITLES AVAILABLE

SOLO SCENES SERIES

THE SIEVE and **CABBAGE** provide invaluable monologue material with a wide variety of theatrical applications and are valid for LAMDA Junior Acting examinations. These short original scenes are proving popular for use with speech and drama pupils in the 8-14 year age range and beyond.

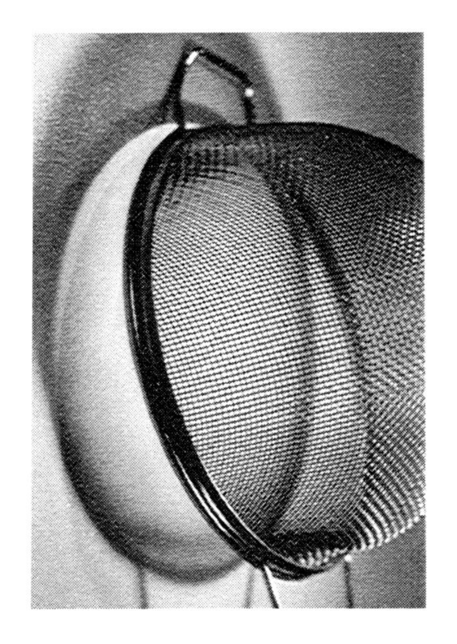

THE SIEVE AND OTHER SCENES
The first book
of original monologues
by Heather Stephens including
an adaptation of
THE LITTLE MATCH GIRL

THE SIEVE AND OTHER SCENES
ISBN 0 9522224 0 X

CABBAGE AND OTHER SCENES
The second book
of original monologues
by Heather Stephens including
an adaptation of
THE PIED PIPER OF HAMELIN

CABBAGE AND OTHER SCENES
ISBN 0 9522224 5 0

DUOLOGUES AND ONE ACT PLAYS

PEARS provides original acting material for two and includes adaptations of scenes from Aristophanes classic play Peace and Dickens Oliver Twist. The scenes are suitable for pupils in the 8-14 year age range and beyond.

PEARS DUOLOGUES
The first book
of original scenes for two
by Heather Stephens

PEARS DUOLOGUES
ISBN 0 9522224 6 9

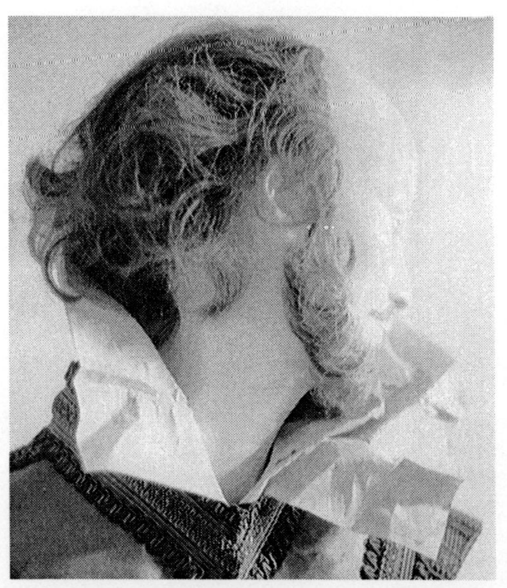

WILL SHAKESPEARE-SAVE US!
WILL SHAKESPEARE-SAVE THE KING!
Two one act plays by Paul Nimmo
in which famous speeches and scenes
from Shakespeare are acted out
as part of a comic story.

WILL SHAKESPEARE-SAVE US!
WILL SHAKESPEARE-SAVE THE KING!
ISBN 0 9522224 1 8

WILL SHAKESPEARE is suitable for performance by a large or small cast aged 11 years upwards and equally suitable for theatre group performance to young people.